Microeconomics for Managers

Roggie Clark

Avoid Credit Card Debt With This Book

Are you tired of living paycheck to paycheck? Drowning in interest rates and minimum payments that never seem to shrink your balance? *Understanding & Overcoming Credit Card Debt* is your roadmap to financial freedom.

https://www.amazon.com/dp/B0F3WCVWG8

Avoid Wasting Money On Crypto With This Book

Whether you're curious, cautious, or ready to invest, this book breaks down complex topics into plain language and cuts through the noise, buzzwords, and get-rich-quick schemes.

https://www.amazon.com/Think-Before-You-Crypto-Understanding-ebook/dp/B0F3YQ1L2Q

Learn How To Invest in Gold Bars With This Book

Whether you're new to investing or seeking to diversify your portfolio, this beginner-friendly guide will give you the knowledge and confidence to invest in gold, and other precious metals.

https://www.amazon.com/Ultimate-Investing-Buying-Guide-Beginners-ebook/dp/B0F1KWWDXG

Learn How To Invest in Silver With This Book

Whether you're approaching retirement or already enjoying it, protecting and growing your wealth is critical. The Ultimate Silver Investing & Buying Guide For Beginners is your clear, no-nonsense guide to incorporating silver into your wealth-building strategy.

https://www.amazon.com/Ultimate-Silver-Investing-Buying-Beginners-ebook

Copyright

Title: Microeconomics for Managers
Author: Roggie Clark

Disclaimer

The views and opinions expressed in this book are those of the author and do not necessarily reflect the official policy or position of any individual, company, or organization cited or referenced in the text. The author is not affiliated with any of the individuals, companies, or organizations mentioned in the text, nor does the author receive any form of compensation for citing or referencing them.

The professional information in this text is distributed on an "as is" basis, without warranty. While every precaution has been taken in the preparation of the text, neither the author nor the publisher shall have any liability to any person or entity with respect to any loss or damage caused or alleged to be caused directly or indirectly by the instructions contained in this text or by the computer software and hardware products described in it.

The author nor the publisher does not guarantee any specific results or outcomes, and the information provided in this text should not be construed as professional advice. Readers should always consult with a qualified professional before making any significant changes to their website or business.

By reading this text, you agree that the author nor the publisher is responsible for any direct, indirect, incidental, or consequential damages that may arise from the use of the information provided. You assume full responsibility for any actions taken based on the information presented in this text.

Table of Contents

Introduction

Microeconomics is often introduced as a subject filled with graphs, formulas, and theories that feel distant from real life. For many people, it becomes something to memorize rather than something to use. But in reality, microeconomics is not just an academic discipline, it is a way of thinking that directly shapes everyday business decisions. Whether you realize it or not, every time you set a price, evaluate a cost, respond to a competitor, or try to understand your customers, you are engaging in microeconomic thinking.

Why This Book Exists

The problem with most explanations of microeconomics is not that they are wrong, it is that they are not practical. They often focus on ideal scenarios, perfect models, and assumptions that rarely exist in the real world. Managers, on the other hand, operate in environments filled with uncertainty, limited information, and constant pressure to make decisions quickly.

This book was created to bridge that gap.

Instead of treating microeconomics as a subject to study, this book treats it as a tool to use. The goal is to help you understand how economic forces influence your decisions and how you can use that understanding to make better choices in real business situations.

Microeconomics as a Decision-Making Tool

At its core, microeconomics is about choices. It examines how individuals and businesses allocate limited resources to achieve specific goals. For managers, those goals often include increasing revenue, controlling costs, improving efficiency, and staying competitive.

Every decision you make has tradeoffs.

- Setting a higher price may increase profit per sale but reduce demand
- Expanding production may increase revenue but also increase costs
- Offering more features may improve customer satisfaction but reduce margins

Microeconomics provides a framework for thinking through these tradeoffs clearly. It helps you move from guessing to reasoning, from reacting to anticipating, and from uncertainty to structured decision-making.

What Makes This Book Different

This book does not assume you want to become an economist. It assumes you want to become a better decision-maker.

You will not be overwhelmed with complex formulas or unnecessary theory. Instead, you will learn concepts in a way that directly connects to real business situations. Each idea is explained with a focus on how it applies to pricing, customer behavior, cost management, competition, and strategy.

The emphasis is on clarity and usefulness.

Rather than asking you to think like a student, this book encourages you to think like a manager who understands how markets actually behave. That includes recognizing that customers are not always rational, competitors do not always act predictably, and outcomes are rarely as clean as a model might suggest.

Who This Book Is For

This book is designed for managers, business owners, team leaders, and professionals who want to make better decisions without getting lost in academic theory.

It is especially useful if you:

- Make pricing or budgeting decisions
- Manage products, services, or teams
- Analyze customer behavior or sales performance
- Want to understand why certain strategies succeed while others fail

You do not need a background in economics to benefit from this book. All you need is a willingness to think more deliberately about the decisions you make.

How to Use This Book

You can approach this book in a way that fits your needs.

If you prefer a structured approach, read it from beginning to end. Each chapter builds on the previous one, helping you develop a stronger and more complete understanding of microeconomic thinking.

If you are focused on solving a specific problem, you can jump to the chapters most relevant to you. Whether you are struggling with pricing, trying to understand customer behavior, or evaluating costs, the concepts in this book are designed to stand on their own while still contributing to a larger framework.

As you read, focus less on memorizing terms and more on understanding ideas. The real value of microeconomics comes from how you apply it, not how well you can define it.

The Bigger Picture

When you begin to see the world through a microeconomic lens, things start to make more sense. Pricing decisions become more intentional. Customer behavior becomes easier to interpret. Business challenges become opportunities to apply structured thinking rather than guesswork.

Over time, this way of thinking compounds.

Small improvements in decision-making can lead to better outcomes, more efficient operations, and stronger strategies. Instead of reacting to changes in the market, you begin to anticipate them. Instead of relying on intuition alone, you combine it with logic and insight.

That is the real advantage this book aims to give you.

Last Thoughts

Microeconomics is not about memorizing curves or formulas, it is about understanding how decisions work in the real world. As a manager, your success is directly tied to the quality of the decisions you make. The better your thinking, the better your outcomes.

This book is your starting point for building that thinking.

As you move forward, focus on applying what you learn, even in small ways. Pay attention to how prices affect behavior, how costs influence strategy, and how customers respond to changes. The more you connect these ideas to your daily decisions, the more valuable they become.

Now that you understand what to expect, let's begin by developing the most important skill in this entire process: learning how to think like a manager, not an economist.

Chapter 1: Thinking Like a Manager, Not an Economist

Microeconomics is often taught as a subject filled with models, assumptions, and theoretical frameworks. While these can be useful, they do not always reflect the reality managers face every day. In business, decisions are made under pressure, with incomplete information, and with real consequences attached. This is why the goal of this chapter is not to turn you into an economist, but to help you think like a manager who uses economic reasoning to make better decisions.

Why Microeconomics Matters for Managers

Every manager makes decisions that are directly tied to microeconomic principles, whether they recognize it or not. Pricing a product, allocating resources, managing supply, and responding to competition all rely on understanding how markets behave.

Microeconomics matters because it provides a structured way to think about these decisions.

Instead of relying purely on intuition or past experience, managers can use economic thinking to evaluate situations more clearly. For example, when deciding whether to increase prices, a manager must consider how customers will respond, how competitors might react, and how the change will affect overall revenue. These are not random guesses, they are microeconomic questions.

Managers who understand these principles are better equipped to:

- Anticipate changes in customer behavior
- Make informed pricing decisions
- Allocate resources more efficiently
- Identify opportunities for growth

Without this understanding, decisions are often reactive rather than strategic.

The Difference Between Theory and Decision-Making

Economic theory is designed to simplify complex realities. It often assumes rational behavior, perfect information, and predictable outcomes. While these assumptions make models easier to understand, they rarely hold true in practice.

Managers operate in a very different environment.

Customers are not always rational. Competitors do not always act predictably. Information is often incomplete, and time constraints force decisions to be made quickly. This creates a gap between theory and real-world decision-making.

Understanding this difference is critical.

Economic theory should be viewed as a guide, not a rulebook. It provides a foundation for thinking, but it must be adapted to fit real situations. For example, a model might suggest that lowering prices will increase demand. While this is often true, it does not account for factors like brand perception, customer loyalty, or market positioning.

A manager must take these additional factors into account.

The goal is not to apply theory blindly, but to use it as a tool for better reasoning.

How Economic Thinking Improves Business Outcomes

Economic thinking helps managers move from guesswork to structured decision-making. It introduces a framework for evaluating tradeoffs, understanding incentives, and predicting outcomes.

One of the most important aspects of economic thinking is recognizing that every decision has an opportunity cost. Choosing one option means giving up another. This applies to everything from pricing strategies to hiring decisions.

For example:

- Investing in marketing may increase demand, but it also reduces available funds for other areas
- Expanding production may increase revenue potential, but it also increases operational complexity
- Lowering prices may boost sales volume, but it may also reduce profit margins

By thinking through these tradeoffs, managers can make more balanced and informed decisions.

Economic thinking also encourages managers to focus on marginal changes. Instead of evaluating decisions in absolute terms, it looks at the additional benefit and cost of each choice. This approach helps managers avoid overcommitting resources and allows for more precise adjustments.

Over time, this leads to better outcomes because decisions are based on logic and analysis rather than impulse.

Common Decision-Making Mistakes Managers Make

Even experienced managers can fall into patterns of thinking that lead to poor decisions. Many of these mistakes occur when economic principles are ignored or misunderstood.

One common mistake is focusing on revenue instead of profit. Increasing sales may seem like a success, but if costs rise faster than revenue, the business may actually lose money.

Another mistake is ignoring customer behavior. Managers may assume that customers will respond predictably to price changes or product updates, only to find that real behavior differs from expectations.

There is also the tendency to rely too heavily on past success. Just because a strategy worked before does not mean it will work in a different market or under different conditions.

Other common mistakes include:

- Overestimating demand
- Underestimating costs
- Failing to consider competitors' responses
- Making decisions based on incomplete data without acknowledging the risk

Recognizing these mistakes is the first step toward avoiding them.

Building a Practical Economic Mindset

Developing an economic mindset does not require advanced mathematics or complex models. It requires a shift in how you approach decisions.

Instead of asking, "What should I do?" a manager with an economic mindset asks:

- What are the tradeoffs?
- How will customers respond?
- What are the costs and benefits?
- What is the likely outcome under different scenarios?

This mindset encourages deliberate thinking.

It also involves being comfortable with uncertainty. Not every decision will have a clear answer, but using economic reasoning can reduce uncertainty and improve the quality of your choices.

Another key aspect is continuous observation. Markets are constantly changing, and managers must adapt. Paying attention to trends, customer behavior, and competitor actions helps refine decision-making over time.

Ultimately, building this mindset is about consistency. The more you apply these principles, the more natural they become.

Last Thoughts

Thinking like a manager, rather than an economist, is about applying economic principles in a practical and flexible way. It is not about memorizing models, but about using structured reasoning to make better decisions in real situations.

As you move forward in this book, keep in mind that the goal is not perfection. You will not always have complete information, and outcomes will not always be predictable. What matters is your ability to think clearly, evaluate tradeoffs, and make decisions with confidence.

By developing this approach, you set the foundation for everything that follows. Each concept you learn will build on this mindset, helping you move from reactive decision-making to a more strategic and intentional way of operating.

With this foundation in place, the next step is to understand one of the most important forces in any market: demand, and how it shapes customer behavior and business decisions.

Chapter 2: Demand, Customers, and Perceived Value

Understanding demand is one of the most important skills a manager can develop. Every business decision, whether it involves pricing, product development, or marketing, is influenced by how customers respond to what you offer. Yet many managers misunderstand demand, treating it as something fixed or predictable. In reality, demand is constantly shifting, shaped by perception, context, and changing customer preferences. This chapter focuses on helping you understand demand in a practical way so you can make better, more informed decisions.

What Demand Really Means in Business

In simple terms, demand refers to how much of a product or service customers are willing and able to buy at different price levels. But in real business environments, demand is not just a number on a chart, it is a reflection of customer interest, perceived value, and purchasing behavior.

Demand is influenced by both willingness and ability.

A customer may want a product but cannot afford it, which limits demand. On the other hand, a customer may be able to afford something but see no value in it, which also reduces demand. True demand exists when both conditions are met.

For managers, this means demand is not something you simply observe, it is something you influence.

How you position your product, communicate its value, and price it all affect how much demand exists in the market. Demand is not just about customers reacting, it is also about how businesses shape those reactions.

Factors That Influence Demand

Demand does not exist in isolation. It is affected by a range of factors that managers must understand in order to make effective decisions.

Price is one of the most obvious factors. As prices increase, demand often decreases, and as prices decrease, demand tends to increase. However, this relationship is not always straightforward.

Customer income also plays a role. When income rises, people may spend more on certain goods and services, increasing demand. When income falls, demand may decrease or shift toward lower-cost alternatives.

Preferences and trends are equally important. Changes in taste, cultural shifts, and emerging trends can significantly impact demand. A product that is popular today may lose demand quickly if consumer preferences change.

Other influencing factors include:

- Availability of substitutes
- Complementary products
- Brand perception and reputation
- Market conditions and external events

Managers must consider all of these factors together rather than relying on a single variable.

Perceived Value vs Actual Value

One of the most important concepts for managers to understand is that customers do not make decisions based solely on actual value, they make decisions based on perceived value.

Actual value refers to the objective benefits a product provides. Perceived value, on the other hand, is how customers interpret those benefits.

For example, two products may have similar features, but if one is branded more effectively or presented as higher quality, customers may perceive it as more valuable and be willing to pay a higher price.

Perception is shaped by:

- Branding and messaging
- Pricing signals
- Customer experience
- Social proof and reputation

This is why demand cannot be fully understood through logic alone. Psychological and emotional factors play a major role in shaping how customers evaluate products.

Managers who understand perceived value can influence demand more effectively. Instead of focusing only on improving the product itself, they can also improve how the product is presented and communicated.

How to Read and Respond to Demand

Reading demand requires more than looking at sales numbers. Sales data shows what has already happened, but managers need to understand why it happened and what is likely to happen next.

One way to interpret demand is to look for patterns.

- Are sales increasing or decreasing over time?
- Do certain price points lead to higher or lower demand?
- Are there seasonal trends or external factors affecting behavior?

Understanding these patterns helps managers anticipate changes rather than react to them.

Responding to demand requires flexibility.

If demand is increasing, managers may need to scale production, adjust pricing, or improve distribution. If demand is decreasing, they may need to reassess pricing, reposition the product, or explore new markets.

It is also important to test and adjust.

Managers should not assume they fully understand demand from the beginning. Instead, they should experiment with pricing, messaging, and product changes to gather insights and refine their approach.

The goal is not to control demand completely, but to respond to it intelligently.

Last Thoughts

Demand is not just a concept, it is a reflection of how customers perceive and respond to your business. Understanding demand allows you to make more informed decisions about pricing, product strategy, and market positioning.

As a manager, your role is not only to observe demand but to influence it. By understanding the factors that drive customer behavior and recognizing the importance of perceived value, you can shape demand in a way that supports your business goals.

As you move forward, keep in mind that demand is always changing. The more closely you pay attention to customer behavior and market signals, the better equipped you will be to adapt and make strategic decisions.

With a clear understanding of demand, the next step is to focus on one of the most critical decisions managers face: pricing, and how it directly impacts revenue and business performance.

Chapter 3: Pricing Decisions and Revenue Strategy

Pricing is one of the most powerful decisions a manager can make. It directly affects revenue, profit, customer perception, and competitive positioning. Yet despite its importance, pricing is often treated as a guess or based on what competitors are doing rather than a structured decision. This chapter focuses on helping you understand pricing as a strategic tool, not just a number attached to a product.

Why Pricing Is Critical

Pricing influences nearly every part of a business.

A small change in price can have a significant impact on revenue and profitability. Increasing prices may improve margins, but it can also reduce demand. Lowering prices may increase sales volume, but it can reduce profit per unit. The balance between these outcomes is what makes pricing such a critical decision.

Pricing also communicates value.

Customers often use price as a signal. A higher price can suggest higher quality, while a lower price may signal affordability or lower value. This means pricing is not just about covering costs, it is also about positioning your product in the market.

Managers who treat pricing as a strategic decision rather than a reactive one are more likely to achieve consistent and sustainable results.

Price Sensitivity and Customer Behavior

Not all customers respond to price changes in the same way. Some are highly sensitive to price, while others are willing to pay more for perceived value, convenience, or brand trust.

Understanding price sensitivity is essential.

If customers are highly sensitive, even a small increase in price can lead to a noticeable drop in demand. On the other hand, if customers are less sensitive, prices can be increased without significantly affecting sales.

Several factors influence price sensitivity:

- Availability of substitutes
- Importance of the product to the customer
- Brand loyalty
- Income levels
- Perceived differences between competing products

For example, customers are generally more sensitive to price changes for non-essential items than for essential goods. A small increase in the price of a luxury item may cause demand to drop significantly, while the same increase for a necessity may have little effect.

Managers must identify how sensitive their customers are before making pricing decisions.

Psychological Pricing

Pricing is not just a mathematical decision, it is also a psychological one.

Customers do not always evaluate prices logically. Instead, they rely on perception, comparison, and emotional responses. This is where psychological pricing comes into play.

One common example is pricing just below a round number. A product priced at 9.99 may feel significantly cheaper than one priced at 10.00, even though the difference is minimal.

Another example is anchoring. When customers see a higher-priced option first, a lower-priced option may appear more attractive by comparison. This technique is often used to guide customer choices.

Perception can also be influenced by how prices are presented:

- Bundling products together
- Offering discounts or limited-time deals
- Highlighting original prices next to discounted prices

These strategies affect how customers interpret value, which in turn affects demand.

Managers who understand psychological pricing can shape customer perception in ways that support their pricing strategy.

Avoiding Pricing Mistakes

Many pricing mistakes occur when decisions are made without fully understanding the underlying factors.

One common mistake is pricing based solely on competitors. While it is important to be aware of the market, blindly matching competitor prices can lead to missed opportunities or reduced profitability.

Another mistake is focusing only on costs. While costs set a baseline, pricing should also reflect the value customers perceive. A product that delivers strong value may justify a higher price, even if production costs are low.

Managers also sometimes lower prices too quickly in response to declining sales. This can train customers to expect discounts and reduce long-term profitability.

Other common mistakes include:

- Ignoring price sensitivity
- Failing to test different pricing strategies
- Overcomplicating pricing structures
- Not adjusting prices as market conditions change

Avoiding these mistakes requires a balanced approach that considers costs, customer behavior, and market conditions.

Last Thoughts

Pricing is not just about setting a number, it is about making a strategic decision that influences how customers perceive your product and how your business performs.

As a manager, your goal is to understand how pricing affects demand, revenue, and profitability, and to use that understanding to make informed decisions. This requires paying attention to customer behavior, testing different approaches, and being willing to adjust as conditions change.

When pricing is approached with intention and insight, it becomes a powerful tool for growth rather than a source of uncertainty.

With a solid understanding of pricing and revenue strategy, the next step is to explore how costs and supply decisions shape profitability and operational efficiency.

Chapter 4: Costs, Supply, and Profit Strategy

Every business decision eventually connects back to costs and supply. While pricing determines how much revenue you bring in, costs and supply determine how much of that revenue you actually keep. Many managers focus heavily on increasing sales, but overlook how cost structures and supply decisions impact profitability. This chapter focuses on helping you understand how costs, supply, and operational decisions work together to shape profit strategy.

Fixed vs Variable Costs

One of the most important distinctions in business is between fixed costs and variable costs.

Fixed costs are expenses that do not change with production levels. These include things like rent, salaries, software subscriptions, and equipment. Whether you produce one unit or one thousand, these costs remain relatively constant in the short term.

Variable costs, on the other hand, change as production increases or decreases. These include materials, shipping, commissions, and other expenses directly tied to output.

Understanding this difference is critical for decision-making.

For example, if a business has high fixed costs, it may need to generate a certain level of sales just to break even. In this case, increasing volume can help spread those fixed costs across more units, improving profitability.

If variable costs are high, increasing production may not significantly improve profit margins, since each additional unit carries a substantial cost.

Managers must evaluate both types of costs together to understand the true financial structure of their business.

Margins and Profitability

Revenue alone does not determine success, profitability does.

Margins represent the difference between revenue and costs, and they are a key indicator of how efficiently a business operates. Even a business with strong sales can struggle if margins are too low.

There are different ways to think about margins, but the core idea is simple: how much profit is generated from each sale.

Managers must consider:

- How much it costs to produce or deliver a product
- How much the product is sold for
- How changes in price or cost affect overall profit

For example, increasing prices may improve margins, but only if demand remains stable. Reducing costs may improve margins, but only if quality and customer satisfaction are not negatively affected.

Profitability is not just about increasing revenue, it is about managing the relationship between revenue and costs effectively.

Capacity and Supply Decisions

Supply is not just about producing goods, it is about managing capacity.

Capacity refers to the maximum level of output a business can sustain. This includes production limits, staffing levels, inventory constraints, and logistical capabilities.

Managers must decide how much to produce and when.

Producing too little can lead to missed sales opportunities and dissatisfied customers. Producing too much can result in excess inventory, increased storage costs, and wasted resources.

Balancing supply with demand is one of the most important operational challenges.

For example:

- A business experiencing high demand may need to increase capacity by hiring more staff or investing in equipment
- A business facing declining demand may need to scale back production to avoid unnecessary costs

Capacity decisions often involve tradeoffs between flexibility and efficiency. Expanding capacity can create growth opportunities, but it also increases risk if demand does not meet expectations.

Aligning Supply With Demand

The goal of supply management is to align production and availability with actual demand.

This requires coordination across multiple areas of the business, including production, inventory, and distribution. Managers must continuously adjust supply based on changing market conditions.

Misalignment between supply and demand can create serious problems.

If supply exceeds demand:

- Inventory builds up
- Costs increase
- Cash flow may be impacted

If demand exceeds supply:

- Sales opportunities are lost
- Customers may turn to competitors
- Brand reputation may suffer

Managers must monitor demand signals and adjust supply accordingly. This may involve scaling production, adjusting pricing, or improving forecasting methods.

Flexibility is key.

Markets change quickly, and supply strategies must be able to adapt. Businesses that can respond quickly to shifts in demand are more likely to maintain efficiency and profitability.

Last Thoughts

Costs and supply are the foundation of profit strategy. While revenue often receives the most attention, it is the management of costs and supply that ultimately determines how successful a business is.

As a manager, your role is to understand how different types of costs affect your decisions, how capacity limits your options, and how supply must be aligned with demand to avoid inefficiencies.

By focusing on margins, managing costs effectively, and making informed supply decisions, you can build a more sustainable and profitable operation.

With a clear understanding of costs and supply, the next step is to explore how elasticity can help you make smarter pricing and revenue decisions.

Chapter 5: Elasticity and Smarter Decision-Making

Not all pricing decisions produce the same results. Sometimes raising prices increases revenue, and other times it causes sales to drop sharply. In some cases, lowering prices boosts total revenue, while in others it simply reduces profit without increasing demand. The difference often comes down to elasticity. Understanding elasticity allows managers to move beyond guesswork and make pricing decisions based on how customers are actually likely to respond.

Understanding Elasticity in Practice

Elasticity measures how sensitive customers are to changes in price.

If a small change in price leads to a large change in demand, the product is considered elastic. If demand changes very little when the price changes, the product is considered inelastic.

While this concept is often explained in theory, its real value comes from how it applies in business decisions.

For example:

- A luxury product with many alternatives is likely to be elastic
- A necessity with few substitutes is more likely to be inelastic

However, elasticity is not fixed. It can change depending on context, timing, and customer perception.

Managers must understand elasticity not as a static number, but as a pattern of behavior that can shift based on how products are positioned and how markets evolve.

When to Raise or Lower Prices

One of the most important uses of elasticity is determining when to adjust prices.

If demand is relatively inelastic, raising prices may increase total revenue because customers continue to buy at similar levels. This is often the case with essential goods or products with strong brand loyalty.

If demand is elastic, raising prices can lead to a significant drop in sales, reducing overall revenue. In these situations, lowering prices may increase sales volume enough to offset the lower price per unit.

The key is understanding how customers will respond before making a change.

Managers should consider:

- How easily customers can switch to alternatives
- How important the product is to the customer
- How the price change will be perceived

Timing also matters.

For example, demand for certain products may become less elastic during peak seasons, allowing for higher prices. Outside of those periods, customers may become more sensitive to price changes.

Revenue Optimization

Elasticity plays a central role in revenue optimization.

The goal is not simply to increase prices or increase volume, but to find the balance that maximizes total revenue while maintaining profitability.

This requires thinking beyond individual sales and focusing on overall outcomes.

For example:

- A higher price with lower volume may generate more profit than a lower price with higher volume
- A lower price may increase customer acquisition, which can lead to long-term value

Managers must evaluate how pricing decisions affect both short-term revenue and long-term strategy.

Testing different pricing strategies can provide valuable insights.

Instead of making large changes all at once, managers can experiment with smaller adjustments to observe how demand responds. This allows for more informed decisions and reduces risk.

Strategic Use of Elasticity

Elasticity is not just a reactive tool, it can also be used strategically.

Managers can influence elasticity through positioning, branding, and product differentiation.

For example:

- Strong branding can reduce price sensitivity by increasing perceived value
- Unique features can make a product less comparable to alternatives
- Bundling products can change how customers evaluate price

By reducing price sensitivity, businesses can gain more flexibility in their pricing strategy.

Elasticity can also inform competitive strategy.

If competitors lower their prices, understanding elasticity helps determine whether matching the price is necessary or whether customers will remain loyal despite the difference.

Ultimately, elasticity helps managers understand the relationship between price, demand, and revenue in a way that supports more strategic decision-making.

Last Thoughts

Elasticity provides a powerful lens for understanding how customers respond to price changes. Instead of relying on assumptions, managers can use elasticity to anticipate reactions and make more informed decisions.

As you apply these concepts, remember that elasticity is not always exact. It is an estimate based on patterns and observations, not a guaranteed outcome. The goal is to use it as a guide for better decision-making rather than a precise formula.

By understanding when to adjust prices, how to optimize revenue, and how to influence customer sensitivity, you can turn pricing into a more strategic and effective tool.

With a strong grasp of elasticity, the next step is to examine how competition and market positioning shape the decisions you make as a manager.

Chapter 6: Competition and Market Positioning

No business operates in isolation. Every decision you make as a manager is influenced not only by your customers, but also by your competitors. Whether you are aware of it or not, your pricing, product strategy, and marketing efforts are constantly being shaped by what other businesses in your market are doing. Understanding competition is not just about watching others, it is about positioning your business in a way that allows you to compete effectively without falling into reactive decision-making.

Competitive Market Dynamics

Competition exists on a spectrum. In some markets, there are many similar businesses offering nearly identical products. In others, a few dominant players control most of the market. The level and type of competition directly influence how you should approach your decisions.

In highly competitive markets, customers have many options. This often increases price sensitivity and makes differentiation more important. In less competitive markets, businesses may have more flexibility in pricing and positioning, but they must still be aware of potential new entrants.

Competition is not just about direct rivals.

It can also come from:

- Substitute products that serve a similar purpose

- New innovations that change customer behavior
- Changes in customer preferences that shift demand away from existing solutions

Managers must broaden their perspective to understand all forms of competition, not just the most obvious ones.

Pricing vs Differentiation

One of the most important strategic decisions managers face is whether to compete on price or differentiation.

Competing on price involves offering lower prices than competitors to attract customers. While this can increase demand, it often leads to lower margins and can trigger price wars that are difficult to sustain.

Differentiation focuses on making your product or service distinct in a way that customers value. This can include quality, branding, customer experience, or unique features.

Differentiation allows businesses to:

- Reduce price sensitivity
- Build customer loyalty
- Justify higher prices

However, differentiation requires consistency. If customers do not clearly understand what makes your product different, they may default to choosing based on price.

Managers must decide which approach aligns with their business model and market conditions.

Responding to Competitors

It is easy for managers to fall into the habit of reacting quickly to competitor actions. If a competitor lowers prices, the instinct may be to do the same. If they launch a new feature, there may be pressure to match it immediately.

However, not every competitor action requires a response.

Reacting without analysis can lead to poor decisions. For example, lowering prices in response to a competitor may reduce profitability without significantly increasing demand.

Instead, managers should ask:

- How will this change actually affect our customers?
- Do we need to respond, or can we maintain our current position?
- Is there an opportunity to differentiate rather than imitate?

Strategic responses are more effective than reactive ones.

Sometimes the best decision is to hold your position and reinforce your value rather than engage in direct competition.

Strategic Positioning

Market positioning is about how your business is perceived relative to competitors. It determines how customers view your product and influences their purchasing decisions.

Positioning is shaped by:

- Pricing
- Branding
- Product features
- Customer experience

A clear position helps customers understand why they should choose your product over others.

For example:

- A premium brand may focus on quality and exclusivity
- A budget brand may focus on affordability and accessibility
- A niche brand may focus on serving a specific audience

Consistency is key.

If your pricing, messaging, and product experience do not align, customers may become confused about your value proposition. This can weaken your position in the market.

Managers must ensure that all aspects of the business support the intended positioning.

Last Thoughts

Competition is not something to fear, it is something to understand and navigate strategically. By recognizing how competitive forces influence your decisions, you can avoid reactive behavior and make more deliberate choices.

As a manager, your goal is not to copy competitors, but to position your business in a way that aligns with your strengths and the needs of your customers. Whether you compete on price, differentiation, or a combination of both, the key is to make intentional decisions rather than impulsive ones.

When you understand competition and positioning, you gain greater control over how your business operates within the market.

With this foundation, the next step is to explore how consumer behavior and psychology influence the decisions customers make, and how those behaviors impact your strategy as a manager.

Chapter 7: Consumer Behavior and Psychology

Understanding demand and pricing is important, but to truly make effective decisions, managers must understand the people behind those numbers. Customers do not always act logically, and their decisions are often influenced by emotions, habits, and perception rather than pure reasoning. This chapter focuses on how consumer behavior and psychology shape purchasing decisions and how managers can use this understanding to improve strategy.

Why Customers Are Not Rational

Traditional economic models often assume that customers act rationally, meaning they always make decisions that maximize their benefit. In reality, this assumption rarely holds true.

Customers are influenced by:

- Emotions
- Habits
- Social pressures
- Limited information

For example, a customer may choose a more expensive product simply because it feels more trustworthy or aligns with their identity. Another customer may avoid switching to a cheaper alternative because they are familiar with a brand and do not want to take a risk.

These behaviors may not appear rational from a purely economic standpoint, but they are very real and predictable in practice.

Managers who assume customers will always act logically often make poor decisions. Recognizing the role of irrational behavior allows managers to better anticipate how customers will actually respond.

Emotional vs Logical Decisions

Most purchasing decisions involve a combination of emotion and logic, but emotion often plays a larger role than expected.

Emotional decisions are driven by feelings such as:

- Trust
- Excitement
- Fear
- Status

Logical decisions are based on measurable factors like price, features, and performance. However, even when customers believe they are making logical decisions, emotion often influences their perception of those factors.

For example:

- A product with strong branding may feel higher quality, even if it is similar to competitors
- A limited-time offer may create urgency, encouraging faster decisions

- Positive reviews may build confidence and reduce hesitation

Managers must understand that appealing only to logic is often not enough. Effective strategies address both emotional and logical drivers.

Substitutes and Decision Drivers

Customers rarely evaluate a product in isolation. They compare it to alternatives, even if those alternatives are not identical.

Substitutes play a major role in shaping decisions.

If customers can easily switch to another option, they are more sensitive to changes in price or value. If there are few alternatives, customers may be more willing to accept higher prices or fewer features.

Decision drivers include:

- Price comparisons
- Convenience
- Brand reputation
- Availability
- Recommendations from others

Understanding these drivers helps managers identify what matters most to customers and how to position their product accordingly.

For example, if convenience is a key driver, improving accessibility may be more effective than lowering price.

Predicting Behavior

While customer behavior is not perfectly predictable, patterns can be observed and used to guide decisions.

Managers can improve their ability to predict behavior by:

- Analyzing past purchasing patterns
- Observing how customers respond to changes
- Testing different strategies and measuring results

For instance:

- If a price increase leads to only a small drop in sales, customers may be less price-sensitive than expected
- If a new feature significantly increases demand, it may indicate strong perceived value

Prediction is not about certainty, it is about improving the likelihood of making the right decision.

The more data and observation managers use, the better their predictions become.

Last Thoughts

Consumer behavior is shaped by more than just price and product features. Emotions, perception, and context all play a role in how customers make decisions.

As a manager, your goal is to understand these influences and use them to guide your strategy. By recognizing that customers are not always rational, you can design pricing, marketing, and product decisions that align with how people actually behave.

The more you understand your customers, the more effectively you can influence demand and improve outcomes.

With a strong understanding of consumer behavior, the next step is to explore how product decisions and value creation influence customer satisfaction and long-term success.

Chapter 8: Product Decisions and Value Creation

Every product decision a manager makes shapes how customers perceive value. While pricing, demand, and competition all play important roles, the foundation of any business is the product or service itself. If the product does not deliver value, no pricing strategy or marketing effort can fully compensate. This chapter focuses on how managers can think about products through the lens of value creation and make decisions that align with customer needs and business goals.

Utility and Customer Satisfaction

At the core of every product decision is utility.

Utility refers to the satisfaction or benefit a customer receives from using a product or service. In simple terms, it answers the question: does this product solve a problem or fulfill a need?

Customers choose products that provide the highest perceived utility relative to their alternatives.

For managers, this means understanding:

- What problem the product solves
- How effectively it solves that problem
- How customers perceive that solution

Utility is not just about functionality. It also includes factors like convenience, design, reliability, and overall experience.

For example:

- A product that saves time may have high utility even if it costs more
- A product that is easy to use may be preferred over a more complex but feature-rich alternative

Managers must focus on delivering value in a way that customers recognize and appreciate.

Feature vs Value Tradeoffs

It is easy to assume that adding more features increases the value of a product. In reality, more is not always better.

Each additional feature comes with tradeoffs:

- Increased production costs
- Greater complexity
- Potential confusion for customers

Managers must evaluate whether new features actually improve perceived value or simply add unnecessary complexity.

For example:

- A simple product that performs one function extremely well may be more valuable than a product with many features that are rarely used

- Too many options can overwhelm customers, making it harder for them to make a decision

The goal is to focus on features that matter most to customers rather than trying to offer everything.

Understanding what customers truly value allows managers to prioritize effectively.

Diminishing Returns

The concept of diminishing returns applies not only to production but also to product development.

As more resources are invested into improving a product, the additional benefit gained from each improvement often decreases.

For example:

- The first improvement to a product may significantly increase customer satisfaction

- Later improvements may have only a small impact

At some point, the cost of adding new features or enhancements may outweigh the value they provide.

Managers must recognize when additional investment is no longer producing meaningful returns.

This requires balancing:

- The cost of development
- The impact on customer satisfaction
- The potential effect on demand

By identifying the point of diminishing returns, managers can allocate resources more efficiently and avoid overinvesting in areas that do not significantly improve value.

Product Strategy Alignment

Product decisions should not be made in isolation. They must align with overall business strategy, pricing, and market positioning.

For example:

- A premium product should deliver a level of quality and experience that justifies a higher price
- A budget product should focus on efficiency and affordability

If product features, pricing, and positioning are not aligned, customers may become confused or dissatisfied.

Alignment also involves understanding the target customer.

Managers must consider:

- Who the product is designed for
- What that customer values most

- How the product compares to alternatives in the market

A clear and consistent product strategy helps ensure that all decisions support the same goal.

Last Thoughts

Product decisions are ultimately decisions about value. The success of a product depends on how well it meets customer needs and how clearly that value is communicated.

As a manager, your role is to focus on what truly matters to customers and make decisions that enhance their experience while maintaining efficiency and profitability.

By understanding utility, managing feature tradeoffs, recognizing diminishing returns, and aligning product strategy with business goals, you can create products that stand out in the market.

With a strong foundation in product decisions and value creation, the final step is to bring all of these concepts together and apply them to real-world business decision-making.

Chapter 9: Making Better Business Decisions With Microeconomics

All of the concepts covered in this book, demand, pricing, costs, elasticity, competition, and consumer behavior, are not meant to exist in isolation. In real business situations, these forces interact at the same time. Managers are rarely faced with simple, one-variable decisions. Instead, they must evaluate multiple factors, often with incomplete information, and still move forward with confidence. This chapter focuses on bringing everything together so you can apply microeconomic thinking in a practical and consistent way.

Bringing Everything Together

Effective decision-making requires connecting concepts rather than treating them separately.

For example, a pricing decision is not just about price. It involves:

- Understanding demand and how customers will respond
- Evaluating costs and margins
- Considering competitor pricing
- Assessing perceived value

Each of these elements influences the outcome.

Managers who isolate decisions often miss important connections. A price increase may look beneficial from a cost perspective, but harmful from a demand perspective. A product improvement may increase value, but also increase costs beyond what customers are willing to pay.

The goal is to view decisions holistically.

Instead of asking a single question, managers should ask multiple related questions:

- How will this affect demand?
- What are the cost implications?
- How will competitors respond?
- What does this mean for long-term strategy?

By connecting these factors, decisions become more balanced and informed.

Decision-Making Frameworks

Having a consistent framework helps managers approach decisions more effectively.

One simple framework involves four steps:

1. Define the Objective
   Clearly identify what you are trying to achieve. This could be increasing revenue, improving margins, gaining market share, or enhancing customer satisfaction.

2. Identify Key Variables
   Determine the factors that will influence the

outcome, such as price, demand, costs, and competition.

3. Evaluate Tradeoffs
   Consider the benefits and costs of each option. Recognize that improving one area may create challenges in another.

4. Make and Monitor the Decision
   Implement the decision and observe the results. Use feedback to refine your approach over time.

This structured approach reduces uncertainty and helps managers avoid impulsive decisions.

Opportunity Cost and Tradeoffs

Every decision involves opportunity cost.

Opportunity cost is the value of the next best alternative that you give up when making a choice. It is often overlooked, but it plays a critical role in decision-making.

For example:

- Investing in one project means not investing in another
- Allocating budget to marketing means less available for operations
- Lowering prices may increase sales but reduce margins

Managers must think beyond the immediate outcome and consider what is being sacrificed.

Tradeoffs are unavoidable.

The goal is not to eliminate tradeoffs, but to choose the option that provides the greatest overall benefit given the circumstances.

Understanding opportunity cost helps managers make decisions that are aligned with long-term goals rather than short-term gains.

Applying Microeconomics Daily

Microeconomic thinking is most valuable when it becomes part of your daily decision-making process.

This does not require complex calculations. It involves consistently asking better questions and evaluating situations more carefully.

In practice, this might look like:

- Reviewing how price changes affect customer behavior
- Monitoring costs and identifying areas for improvement
- Observing competitor actions and evaluating their impact
- Adjusting strategies based on market feedback

Over time, these small, consistent actions lead to better outcomes.

Managers who apply microeconomic thinking regularly develop stronger intuition, not because they rely on instinct alone, but because their intuition is informed by structured reasoning.

This creates a powerful advantage.

Last Thoughts

Making better business decisions is not about having perfect information, it is about using the information you have more effectively. Microeconomics provides a framework for thinking through complex situations, evaluating tradeoffs, and making decisions with greater clarity.

As a manager, your ability to think critically and apply these concepts will directly influence your results. The more you practice this approach, the more confident and consistent your decision-making will become.

This book is not meant to be read once and forgotten. It is meant to be used as a reference and a guide as you navigate real business challenges.

By applying microeconomic thinking to your daily decisions, you position yourself to make smarter choices, adapt to changing conditions, and lead with greater confidence and effectiveness.

You now have the foundation. What matters most is how you use it.

Closing

Microeconomics is often introduced as a subject to learn, but as you have seen throughout this book, its real value comes from how it is applied. Every concept we covered, from demand and pricing to costs, competition, and consumer behavior, is directly connected to the decisions managers make every day. These are not abstract ideas. They are practical tools that shape outcomes in real business environments.

Bringing It All Together

At its core, microeconomics is about understanding how decisions work.

Every decision you make involves tradeoffs. You are constantly balancing price and demand, cost and value, short-term results and long-term strategy. The more clearly you understand these relationships, the more confident and effective your decisions become.

What separates strong managers from average ones is not access to more information, but the ability to interpret and act on the information they have.

By applying microeconomic thinking, you:

- Move from guessing to structured reasoning
- Anticipate outcomes instead of reacting to them
- Make decisions that align with both customer behavior and business goals

This shift in thinking is where real progress happens.

The Power of Consistent Application

The concepts in this book are most powerful when used consistently.

You do not need to apply everything at once. Instead, focus on small improvements in how you approach decisions. Pay attention to how customers respond to pricing changes. Evaluate how costs impact your margins. Observe how competitors influence your positioning.

Over time, these observations build a stronger understanding of how your business operates.

Consistency leads to clarity.

The more you apply these principles, the more natural they become. What once required careful thought becomes part of how you approach problems automatically.

Thinking Beyond the Book

No book can account for every situation you will face as a manager. Markets change, customer preferences evolve, and new challenges emerge. However, the framework you have developed here will help you adapt.

Instead of relying on fixed answers, you now have a way to think through problems.

When faced with a decision, you can ask:

- What are the tradeoffs?
- How will customers respond?

- What are the costs and benefits?
- How does this affect long-term strategy?

These questions guide you toward better outcomes, even in uncertain situations.

Final Thoughts

Success in management is not about avoiding mistakes, it is about making better decisions over time. Microeconomic thinking gives you the tools to do exactly that.

As you move forward, remember that every decision is an opportunity to apply what you have learned. The more intentional you are in your thinking, the more effective your actions will be.

This is not the end of the process, it is the beginning of a new way of approaching decisions.

You now have a framework. Use it.

Glossary

Understanding key terms is important, but in this book, the goal is not just to define them, it is to understand how they apply to real decisions. Below are the core microeconomic concepts you encountered, explained in a clear and practical way.

Demand

The quantity of a product or service that customers are willing and able to buy at different price levels. In practice, demand reflects customer interest, perceived value, and purchasing behavior.

Supply

The quantity of a product or service that a business is willing and able to offer at various price levels. Supply is influenced by production capacity, costs, and operational decisions.

Market Equilibrium

The point where supply and demand are balanced, meaning the quantity supplied equals the quantity demanded. In real business settings, this is often a moving target rather than a fixed point.

Price Sensitivity

The degree to which customers respond to changes in price. High sensitivity means customers are likely to change their behavior when prices change, while low sensitivity means they are less affected.

Elasticity

A measure of how much demand changes in response to price changes. It helps managers understand whether raising or lowering prices will likely increase or decrease revenue.

Inelastic Demand

A situation where demand changes very little when the price changes. This often applies to essential goods or products with strong brand loyalty.

Elastic Demand

A situation where demand changes significantly when the price changes. This is common for non-essential products or those with many alternatives.

Utility

The satisfaction or value a customer receives from a product or service. Utility is subjective and varies between individuals.

Perceived Value

How customers interpret the value of a product based on factors like branding, pricing, and experience. This often has a greater impact on decisions than actual value.

Opportunity Cost

The value of the next best alternative that is given up when making a decision. Every choice involves a tradeoff.

Marginal Thinking

The process of evaluating the additional benefit and cost of making one more unit of a decision. This helps managers make more precise and efficient choices.

Fixed Costs

Costs that do not change with production levels, such as rent, salaries, and equipment expenses.

Variable Costs

Costs that change based on production or sales volume, such as materials, shipping, and commissions.

Profit Margin

The difference between revenue and costs, expressed as a percentage or amount. It reflects how efficiently a business converts sales into profit.

Capacity

The maximum level of output a business can sustain given its resources, including labor, equipment, and infrastructure.

Substitutes

Products or services that can replace one another. When substitutes are available, customers are more likely to switch if prices or value change.

Differentiation

The process of making a product or service distinct from competitors in a way that customers value, such as through quality, branding, or features.

Market Positioning

How a product or brand is perceived relative to competitors. Positioning influences customer expectations and purchasing decisions.

Consumer Behavior

The study of how customers make purchasing decisions, including the role of emotions, preferences, and external influences.

Psychological Pricing

Pricing strategies designed to influence perception, such as pricing just below a round number or using discounts to create urgency.

Revenue

The total amount of money generated from sales before costs are deducted.

Profit

The amount of money remaining after all costs are subtracted from revenue.

Tradeoffs

The balancing of benefits and costs when making a decision. Improving one area often requires sacrificing another.

Last Thoughts

The purpose of this glossary is not just to help you recognize terms, but to reinforce your understanding of how these concepts connect to real decisions. As you continue to apply what you have learned, these ideas will become more than definitions, they will become part of how you think.

The more familiar you are with these concepts, the easier it becomes to approach decisions with clarity and confidence.

About the Author

Roggie “Raj” Clark is an entrepreneur, author, and education minded creator whose work spans digital marketing, investing, economics, programming, and early academic development. With more than a decade of experience in ecommerce and digital business growth, he has built and managed successful online stores with thousands of sales and consulted for numerous marketing clients on branding, consumer behavior, and online strategy.

As a former marketing manager at a fintech company, Roggie gained firsthand experience in financial systems, wealth building strategy, and economic decision making. That experience inspired him to write books focused on investing, financial literacy, macro and microeconomics, and helping readers make informed long term financial decisions.

Roggie also holds a degree in Elementary Education and has a background in classroom teaching. Drawing from his academic training and educational experience, he has written classroom aligned books designed to support learning standards and structured skill development. His educational titles are intentionally crafted to blend clear instruction with engaging content that supports both classroom and homeschool learning environments.

Whether explaining search engine optimization, programming concepts such as HTML, CSS, and JavaScript, economic principles, or foundational academic skills, Roggie focuses on breaking complex topics into accessible learning experiences. Across every subject he writes about, his goal is to build strong foundations, encourage critical thinking, and equip readers with tools that support long term growth.

He lives in Maryland and continues to develop educational and business focused resources designed to inform, empower, and inspire.

www.ingramcontent.com/pod-product-compliance
Lightning Source LLC
LaVergne TN
LVHW022315200926
848481LV00004B/1352
9798295762192